Relax and enjoy!

Kumon's First Steps Workbooks are designed so that children and parents can learn and have fun together. Children learn best from active and participatory parents, so please help your child with the activities in this book. By helping, you are encouraging your child to develop a desire to learn, as well as laying the foundation for him or her to become a self-motivated learner.

How to choose and hold scissors

Scissors can be dangerous if not handled properly. Keep an eye on your child when he or she is doing the cutting exercises.

How to choose a good pair of scissors

1 Choose safety scissors with round tips.

2 Choose scissors with holes that suit your child's hands and fingers.

3 Choose scissors your child can open and close easily.

▲ Please choose easy-to-use safety scissors. Pictured on the right are plastic safety scissors.

How to hold scissors properly

Show your child how to put his or her thumb into the smaller hole and his or her forefinger and middle finger into the bigger hole of the scissors. If the bigger hole is large enough, have your child put his or her ring finger into the hole as well.

When your child holds scissors, please align his or her hand with the scissors so that they form a straight line when viewed from above.

▲ Please try to align your c[...]
scissors so that they form [...]

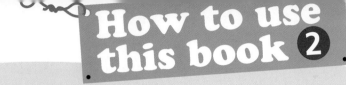

How to cut with scissors

Show your child how to cut along the designated lines. It is perfectly okay if your child cannot cut completely accurately. He or she will gradually learn to do so.

The first step in cutting is learning how to properly manipulate scissors. Check to see if your child can easily open and close the scissors, and also check to see if he or she can hold the scissors at a right angle to the paper.

▲ In the early stages, children usually cut unevenly.

Encourage your child to align the scissors with the cutting line. Please do not be concerned if your child cuts off of the designated line, or if he or she cannot stop the scissors at a designated point.

▲ Cutting a rectangular line can be difficult.

Show your child how to hold the paper away from the scissors, with the scissors pointed at the cutting line. This is a difficult skill that requires some getting used to.

Tips for cutting neatly
Open the scissors wide and cut half an inch, then open the scissors wide again and cut another half an inch. Repeat this technique.

▲ In order to cut neatly, use the section of the blades nearest to the joint in the scissors.

16 **Digging Mole**

Done!

To parents
When your child is finished cutting along the designated line, pretend to dig in the ground like the mole.

Cut along ▬▬▬.

✂ Parents: Please cut along ▬▬▬ for your child.

mole

17 Crocodile and Friend

Done!

Cut along .

✄ Parents: Please cut along ▬▬▬ for your child.

crocodile

Wild Boar

Done!

Cut along ▭.

✂ Parents: Please cut along ▬▬▬ for your child.

wild boar

20 Camel

Done!

To parents
Help your child open and close the scissors with short strokes in order to cut curves neatly. Through repeated practice, he or she will acquire firm scissor control.

Cut along 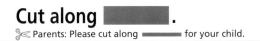.

✂ Parents: Please cut along ▬▬▬ for your child.

camel

Whale
Jumping Frogs

Done!

To parents
In this exercise, your child needs to hold the paper and turn it while cutting. Make sure he or she is holding the scissors at the proper angle. Through repeated practice, he or she will acquire firm scissor control.

Cut along [____].

✄ Parents: Please cut along ▬▬▬ for your child.

frog

Done!

To parents
If your child seems to be having difficulty cutting along the designated line, offer your help. Have fun fishing!

Cut along [   ].

✂ Parents: Please cut along ▬▬▬ for your child.

fish

27 Squirrel's Swirly Tail

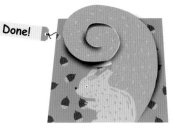
Done!

To parents
In this exercise, your child will hold the paper and rotate it in order to cut in a circular direction. Do not be concerned if your child's cutting is crooked. The most important thing is that your child enjoys cutting paper.

Cut along ▬▬▬▬.

✂ Parents: Please cut along ▬▬▬ for your child.

squirrel

28 **Springing Snake**

To parents
The cutting line in this exercise is more difficult to cut than in previous pages. When your child finished, offer lots of praise.

Cut along 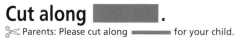.

✂ Parents: Please cut along ▬▬▬ for your child.

snake

29 Chameleon

Done!

To parents
Have fun twisting the chameleon's tail around your child's finger.

Cut along ▬▬▬.

✂ Parents: Please cut along ▬▬▬ for your child.

chameleon

30 Cat

Done!

To parents
From this page on, your child will practice cutting out the figures from the
edge of the page. When your child has finished, pretend to be the cat
and say something like, "Meow. I'm so sleepy!"

Cut along 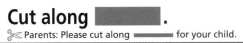.

✂ Parents: Please cut along ▬▬▬ for your child.

cat

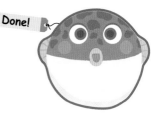

Done!

To parents
In this exercise, your child will practice rotating the paper while cutting in order to cut evenly curved lines.

Cut along ▬▬▬.

✂ Parents: Please cut along ▬▬▬ for your child.

puffer fish

32 **Hermit Crab**

Done!

Cut along ▬▬▬.

✂ Parents: Please cut along ▬▬▬ for your child.

hermit crab

Done!

To parents
If your child is cutting off the line, help him or her adjust the direction of the scissors. If your child accidentally cuts into the illustration, just repair it with tape.

Cut along 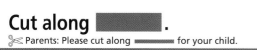.

✂ Parents: Please cut along ▬▬▬ for your child.

gorilla

↑

To parents
It is okay for your child to close the scissors completely with every stroke if he or she seems to be able to control the scissors well.

Cut along 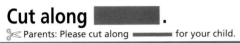.

✂ Parents: Please cut along ▬▬▬ for your child.

turtle

35 Pig

To parents
If your child does not cut perfectly, that is okay. It's more important that your child enjoys cutting.

Cut along .

Parents: Please cut along for your child.

pig

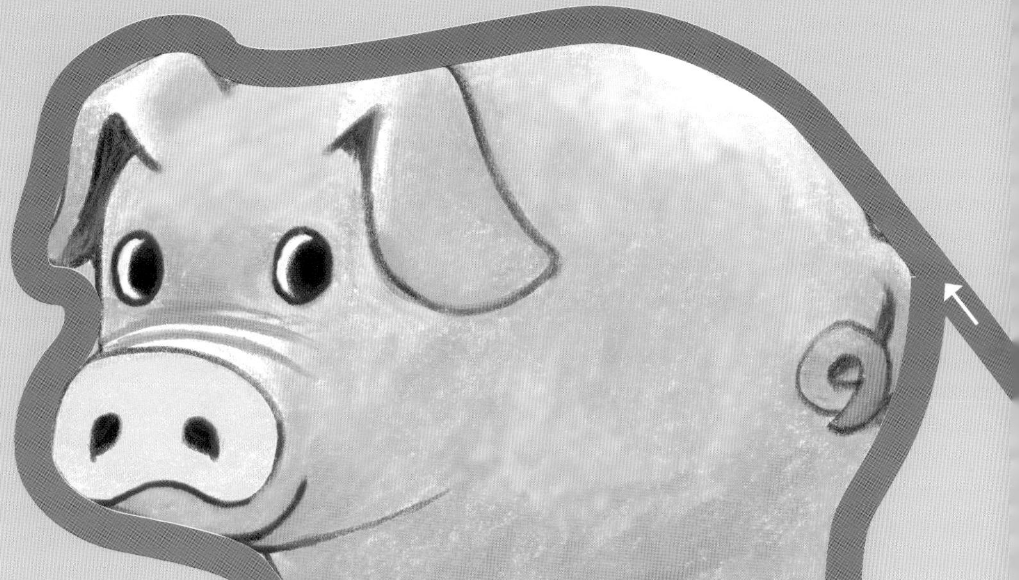

36 **Bunny Hop**

Done!

To parents
The designated line here is more difficult than in previous exercises. When your child has successfully cut out the bunny, please offer lots of praise.

Cut along 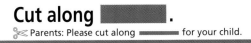.

✂ Parents: Please cut along ▬▬▬ for your child.

bunny

Done!

Cut along ▬▬▬ .

✂ Parents: Please cut along ▬▬▬ for your child.

sheep

38 Chicken

Done!

Cut along .

✂ Parents: Please cut along ▬▬▬ for your child.

chicken

39 Dog

To parents
This is the last exercise in this workbook. Compare your child's work on this exercise with his or her earlier work. You will probably notice a lot of progress in your child's ability to cut paper precisely. Offer lots of praise for his or her accomplishment!

Cut along 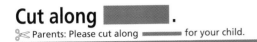.

✂ Parents: Please cut along ▬▬▬ for your child.

dog

KUM◯N

Certificate of Achievement

is hereby congratulated on completing

Let's Cut Paper! Amazing Animals

Presented on _____ , 20 ____

_____
Parent or Guardian